# Goldfish

*Dan, I hope you enjoy the read!*

*Jon Aylett*

Jonathan Aylett

Stairwell Books //

Published by Stairwell Books
161 Lowther Street
York, YO31 7LZ

www.stairwellbooks.co.uk
@stairwellbooks

ISBN: 978-1-913432-91-1
p5

Cover Art: © Eden Mullane

For Antoinette

# Table of Contents

# BEAUTIFUL CHAOS

fleeting glimpses –
memories, dressed as goldfish
in the murky depths

## Life in a Goldfish bowl is all well and good, but only if your attention span is 2 seconds or shorter

So follow the cruisers
Come, do what they're doing
Ignore all your bruises
and go where they're going
To see what they're seeing!
To know what they're knowing!
With this scheme they're scheming
This seed they're sowing
which grows in your mind
on the thoughts that you've borrowed
But what will you find
when it comes to tomorrow?
Will you wake up blind
with no-one to follow
and a heart all caught up
in a feeling like sorrow?
Will you curse your bad luck
and wish you could see them,
just to drink from their cup,
feel that love-lustre feeling?
Or will you wake up
with a sense you're still dreaming?
Will you think
you can tell
that it's not what it's seeming
while deep down, you know
you can scarce shake the feeling?
Or just lie there
and stare
at the cracks in the ceiling?

Their faces are there
and they're beckoning to you
Saying "Climb up again
and let us all screw you..."
You crawl through the crack,
it's a squeeze, but you make it
You're burning with thirst
and you're yearning to slake it

Just
  one
    more
       hit...

and then you'll forsake it
One more sight of their light
One more glimmering night
One more taste of their grace
One more dose of their favour
One more bite, one more slice
One more morsel to savour
*(Don't fight, it's alright –*
*you get used to the flavour)*
One more spin of the wheel
One more day in the sun
You can't say, you just feel
like your time has begun

You return to the fairground
the high helter-skelter
But all that remains
is a smashed-up bus shelter
The glitter-ball halls
and fairy-light valleys

are crumbling walls
and needle-strewn alleys
You wander down hallways
through myriad mazes
Past passages, crawl-ways
and all kinds of places
You visit the floors
of the clubs and the bars
The guys on the doors
don't know where they are
All they can say
of the people you seek
Is "They were here yesterday,
or maybe last week…"
But you're not giving up
You're filled with a craving
You had your first sup
and your mind's set to raving
So you run through the dust
that lies trailing behind them
You look, *(well you must)*
but you can't seem to find them
and just when you think
that it isn't worth chasing
When your feet are worn down
and your heartbeat's racing
They stop
and they turn
and they say
"We've been waiting."
and "Where have you been?"
and "How are you doing?"
While they're opening doors
and ushering you in

So you've got it
You've found what
you think you've been needing
While they kick you
and stick you
to see that you're bleeding
and you don't realise
it's on you that they're feeding
These people so fine,
these people so pretty
with their cigarettes, wine
with the curls in their hair
who give you their time
*(while you've money to spare)*
Who give you their voices
their laughter so hollow
till your head starts spinning
you can't seem to swallow
Till your knees feel weak
and your toes go numb
you're trying to speak
but the words won't come
The air you were breathing
has turned into treacle
The path you were cleaving
is choked with these people
whose flashing white smiles
are searing your eyes
While your ears are unhearing
to all but their lies
Till it all gets too much
you can't take any more
and you don't even know it
when you fall to the floor

You lie at their feet
and you stare up around them
Through the cold, hard light
that seems to surround them
The glaring reflections
which shine from their surface,
deflecting detection
without any purpose
Directing attention
at their shimmering skin
Neglecting to mention
there's nothing within
Striking all types
of improbable poses
Harvesting likes
with photoshopped noses
and six packs
and thigh gaps
and paid partnerships
and links in the bio
for life-hacks, and tips
Selling the dream
that it isn't all lies
that it is what it seems
*(but you need to subscribe)*
This beautiful tribe
thinking pre-packaged thoughts
Appearing to thrive
in the web that they're caught
Trapped in the tracks
of a tape loop, a rosary
Insatiably chasing
the thumbs-up emoji
So carefully carefree,

so fucking fantastic!
Living their best lives
as single-use plastic
Inventing themselves
making myths of their sins
Inflating their egos
by sucking you in

You crawl to the wall
on your hands and your knees
You prop yourself up
but nobody sees
Nobody cares
if you're whole
or you're healthy
They're all way too busy
posing for selfies
Completely cut off
from other folk's troubles
Hermetically sealed
in their own little bubbles
With faces lit up
by the gleam
of their screens
They scroll past the bits
that they don't want to see
and move on to the next one
The next you,
the next me
Unable to tell
the fake from the real
Racing, pell-mell
on a gold hamster wheel
Always in motion

just look at them go!
Pushing the notion
that they're in the know
That they are the ones
who are living the dream
and to be just like them
is the best thing to be

A thought starts to bud
in the back of your mind
A strand which you tug
for an answer to find
You pull on that thread,
though you fear it may snap
This idea in your head
drags you out of the trap
And you suddenly see
why they seek adulation
They're just stemming the tide
of their own desperation
Prolonging the ride
with self-medication
Numbing the pain
of a vacant vocation
with spirals of
knock-you down
spin-you-round
pick-me-ups
Counterfeit people
devouring barbiturates
With no room
for the negative
That simply won't do!
Just pop a quick sedative

to get yourself through
and return, reinstated
in a positive light
The dark, not negated
just kept out of sight

A rumble starts growing,
the faintest of sounds
A tremor that's building
in the walls and the ground
And it's snowballing
steamrolling
up to a shout
So you stamp
and you scream
and you yell
LET ME OUT!
Then, just like that
the notes fall flat
the band stops swaying
the music stops playing
the disco ball falls
to the floor with a jolt
The carousel stalls
to a juddering halt
The smiles and the crowns
on the marionettes
have all turned to frowns
pale masks of regret
Nobody's speaking,
nobody's moving
no waking
no sleeping
no begging

no choosing
no taking
no giving
no laughing
no crying
There's no more living
and no more dying
All you can hear
is a hollow wind sighing
As the shadows around you
tremble and fade

(Epilogue)

You dust yourself off
as the mist drifts away
You open your eyes
in the cold light of day
and you're back in your room
still there on your bed
The cracks in the plaster
still hang overhead
and you think to yourself
as you yawn and you stretch
It was only a dream
and pretty far-fetched
and you're glad
you're not one
of those people
so tasteless
as you reach for your phone
and update your status

light, dark, endless arc
flip side of a twisted strip
a new dawn rises

# Ode to Nowhere

No destination on this trip,
we ride a rolling
Möbius strip
The life we seek
always in sight,
just out of reach
This is our plight
To yearn for things
we cannot grasp
To clutch and cling
for what won't last
To dream of what
might come to pass
The other side
that greener grass
We glimpse it from
this wave we surf
not knowing that
it's astroturf
Yet mesmerised
we struggle on
we fight the tide
we slip
we slide
We long to fly
in bluer skies
We never stop
to wonder why
So, on we rush
through light and dark
Sleepwalking through
our boundless arc

Each day a treasure
cast aside
Lives unmeasured
trapped inside
the tape loop
of our daily grind
Oblivious
preoccupied
with paying pipers
keeping time
We chase our tails
We toe the line
And through the window
rushing by
The flowers grow,
and bloom
and die

fully committed
to life in the fast lane –
wing mirror spider

# Anachronism in the UK

Punk is not dead...
It just lost a little steam
After all, it was only
a youthful dream
and as it turns out
not quite what it seemed
So while I always was inclined
to agree
that the queen
weren't no human being
and one glance
at the news
makes it pretty bloody obvious
for anyone to see
that we truly are living
in a fascist regime
I just can't be arsed anymore
to dye my hair green
hang around the town
be part of that scene
I've traded coke and JD
for tea and bourbon creams
and now I just stay in
forget about the glamour
put my feet up
have a snooze
or watch homes
     under
         the hammer...

Punk hasn't died…
It just started
to st-stutter
but it's still there, if you look
growling at you
from the gutter
And yeah OK, I know that
Johnny Rotten's
done that stuff on telly
flogging butter
But he's just a celebrity now
get him out of here!
He's gone from ginger nutter
to soggy custard cream
dunking himself
in controversy
desperate for publicity
It made him a moron
and when all's said and done
it never was about him
it was about kids like you and me
trying to find
an identity
in the cultural desert
of Thatcher's 80s
When join a tribe
to survive
was the only way to be

Punk isn't dead...
but it is middle aged
you can't hear London Calling
when you need a hearing aid
It told us you could always
find it out to lunch
but nowadays it stays at home
watching Bargain Hunt
with crumbs all down it's jumper
from cream crackers that it crunched
So don't ask where it is
you'll get no reply
It might've had no future
but I'm sure it didn't die
Because it's here, you see
buried deep inside
I know I'm not pretty
and I'm increasingly vacant
But spare me your pity
cos I'm the place punk went
and there's always
gonna be
a little bit of me
that will never ever stop
wanting to be
Anarchy

not morning people
lizard basking on a rock
me sipping coffee

# Give it Back

Come on son!
What's the craic?
You've had your fun
Just give it back
After all it's not your ball
Kick it over here where it belongs
Look, I know you think you're
big and strong
But deep down you know
you're in the wrong
So, come on mate
Just give it back
Stop being such a twat

There – that was easy, wasn't it?
I'm sure that if you just learn to behave
the other kids might let you play

So what's stopping us
from giving everything back?

You know what I mean –
The artefacts we took
without asking
marbles crowbarred
from the Parthenon
bronzes from Benin
the Rosetta Stone
all those long dead Egyptian bones
I mean, is that really
who we want to be?
Is this the state of our nation?

Or are childhood lessons not translating?
Sure, treasures can be taken
but culture can never be appropriated
We've got our own, let's own that
and learn to celebrate it
It wasn't Empire that made Britain great
We built Stonehenge for pity's sake!

What would it take
to smash the mould
shrug off our shackles
relinquish claims?
The broken loom
could be remade
These worn out threads
restrung, reframed
and from that fresh-hung
warp and weft
new wisdom would be woven
So nevermore
would we be left
blindfolded and beholden
to misplaced muted memories
or rose-tinted nostalgia
Let's push things forward
peacefully
unbound from our neuralgia
and find a place
where we can face
the dirty rotten truth
Admit that we were
nothing more
than bully boys
and brutes

Give back the stash
which once we snatched
Restore the stolen loot!

Forgiveness isn't ours to give
It seems there's no salvation
But burned-out bridges could be rebuilt
by making reparations
and maybe
on some future day
if we pay our dues
there might be a movie made
where the villain
isn't an Englishman

danger close
they're better off without me
he says to himself

# My mate Dave

My mate Dave
he's a walking cliché
Look, here he is
holding a fish on
his profile pic
(Swipe left)
Our Dave goes to the gym on weekdays,
(only does weights)
He's got a sleeve tattoo and a skin fade,
wears tight t-shirts,
spends Saturday down the footy with his mates.
But that's just modern-day chain mail,
armour for cisgendered white males.
Because where he's from
there's no middle ground
If you don't look like a predator, you'll end up being prey
That don't fuck with me vibe
is how he survived
He learned from an early age
that nice guys never thrive
They end up alone
at the back of the line.
(Or worse, left hanging on in the friend zone)
Boys don't cry
they bottle it inside
and they grow into men like Dave
who are 75% more likely
to die
by suicide

My mate Dave

threw it all away
Stepped out in front of
a Merseyrail train.
(Nobody saw it coming).
He never understood the concept of odds, our Dave
Never realised that nobody wins
except the bookie
He hated the game, but he kept on playing
hoping he might get lucky one day
But Dave's odds were stacked
like a 10-game acca
and now his number's up.

You might have little sympathy
If you've been hurt, or worse
by someone who looks like Dave
And I don't deny
that if that happened, you're entitled to your rage
But paying it forward, that just
perpetuates the cycle
The only way to bring about change
is with love
simply love

Isn't it ironic how often the ones
most in need of that love
are the ones we are least inclined to like?

not quite rock bottom
the moss, living her best life
down in the gutter

# NEURODI-VERSES

all hallow's day
I put away the costume
and replace my mask

# Ode to a co-worker

I heard you
when you said
"He's on the spectrum…"
Covering your mouth
to avoid detection
Acting cool
with your clique
around the cooler
Drinking all the Kool-Aid™
Trying to throw some
casual kind of shade, and
I'm here to let you know
that yeah, OK, I see you
I've got you made
And you're dead right
I am on the spectrum
But all that means is
I'm the rainbow
to your beige
So don't worry,
I'll contain my rage
Cos it's a superpower
not a cage
On the spectrum?
I'm a weapon
Rhymes are my guitar
and my mind's
the plectrum
Let's turn the page
Do you know what it took
for me
to put myself on this stage?

No.
Of course you don't
You're sat at home
without a worry
watching Corrie
eating a curry
and I'm sure that
if I put you on the spot
you would say
that you're sorry
But that's not good enough,
the damage has been done
Not just by you
but by anyone who
ever tried to force me
through the doors
of their preconceptions
Confronted me
with clauses, buried
misdirection in the
hidden meanings
subtle subtext
couched in deception
attempted to arrest
my inevitable
progression
with so very many
teeny-tiny
micro-aggressions

But hey it's ok.
I can see you're getting upset
I'm not going to talk to
Tina in HR (at least not yet)

I've got no time for all
her empty platitudes
and that fake self-serving
middle-management attitude
I don't need
a sympathy vote, or
to tick the box
of a diversity quota
so I'll let you off the
hook, but look, just try to see
me for who I am.
And if that really is beyond
your comprehension
don't try to make sense
of it or label me or respond with
condescension, or put
me in a box or cast
aspersions, just
remember this –
If you've met one
neurodivergent person
Then you've
      met
  One
         NeuRo-
  DiV_erGeNt
      p  e  r  s  o  n

I always felt like
that turned inside-out pinky
in the glove's lining

# Meltdown

It's one of those days when the hatches need battening
so much stimulus rushing in
breaking down the defences my
senses are taking a battering.
Can't stand standing in
queues and the queue jumpers
cutting in
Or shut out the din of the train on the
tracks and the feel of the wheels which
are constantly clattering.
Scratchy socks, tight and hot on my feet.
*Will these passengers ever stop chattering?*
My mind in a mess, tangled
frequencies splitting and scattering.
I'm close to shattering,
not flatlining yet but I feel the line flattening.
The candle burns down,
the flame
is guttering.

*(A tsunami is coming can't stop it from flooding in)*

Here it is –
crashing roaring the wave, uncontrollable
rage, forcing it inwards but still
overwhelmed swept away, helplessly
caught in its
grip defenceless and now my
mask slips... I become
the eye of a storm can't conceal
what's been there all along – that
this face I present

to the world is all wrong
the smile that I keep
drawing on was never a
smile but an
　upside-down
　frown
Greasepaint on a clown
　　I'm lost in a m
　　　　　　e
　　　　　l
　　　　　　t
　　　　　　　d
　　　　　　　　o
　　　　　　　　　w
　　　　　　　　n

still expecting me
to fulfil my potential
Dad's old diary

# Chairman of the drawing board

It seems as though
I'm on a mission
to lay down plans
without fruition
Foiled again
and then once more
I'm trapped
in a revolving door
I take the shot
but never score
I'm the chairman
of the drawing board

Born bereft
of silver spoon
I rose to this position
Sweeping clean
a brand-new broom
breaking with tradition
If you could see
the dreams which bloom
like fleeting apparitions
You'd understand
why I'm consumed
with reaching my ambition
But dreams dissolve
and I'm not sure
that they are destined
to endure
It's all been said
or done before
I'm the chairman
of the drawing board

Yet still I sit
within the gloom
cloistered in
my smallest room
concocting schemes
and half-baked plans
composing tunes
for unknown bands
On ticket stubs
and crumpled scraps
I scribble my prescriptions
There's post it notes
inside my coat
defying all description
and notebooks
full of formulae
which never see
the light of day
They gather dust
and clutter drawers
or sit in stacks
upon the floor
I've told you twice
now one time more
I'm the chairman
of the drawing board

But one day soon
I will complete
my final manifesto
If you would only
hear me out
you might just
be impressed

Oh, but it'll come
as no surprise
to watch your eyes
glaze over
You'll make excuses
turn your backs
I'll get the old
cold shoulder
And as you shuffle
through the door
I'll simply shrug
(I know the score)
It's just my fate
to be ignored
I'm the chairman
of the drawing board

that death-row feeling
the last day of summer break
before school begins

# Chrysalis

I never knew I was a butterfly,
I believed in the stories I'd been told.
That I was born broken, a human child
who never was able to fit the mould.

Scooped up in a net and pinned to a board
by a system designed to reshape me.
Sat at the back, shouted down or ignored,
given chemicals meant to placate me.

But truth can never be buried for long -
if you're patient it comes to the surface.
I began to believe I could belong,
and I'm finally finding my purpose.

At last, I see what has always been there:
I'm a butterfly – I'll take to the air!

it takes grit sometimes
to hold it all together
ask a sandcastle

## There's no such thing as the literary establishment (there's only the establishment)

If you stand at the back on a night like this
If you're screwed up tighter than the paper balled in your fist
If you feel like you're stuck but you think you should twist
If you're wondering whether to give it a go
but you tell yourself no, I'll give it a miss
not right now not this time maybe next week
I'd like to tell you this;
I've been there too,
and I would love to hear you speak
because I can see what you still won't admit
You are a poet

If you wrestle in vain with the blank empty page
If you can't quite find the words to convey all
those things you've been meaning to say
If you never have time
If your mind trips over itself
reaching for rhymes which slip through your fingers
while you pace back and forth like
you're caught in a cage
Relax, disengage – it's a trap of your own design.
Breathe, go outside, put it all to one side.
The words will come in their own good time,
because you are a poet

If you find yourself dejected, another
rejection – words on the
screen stab your eyes pierce your brain like
bayonets to your self-esteem

know this – it's not what it seems
There's no such thing as the literary establishment
there's only the establishment
and hasn't it always been their mission to keep people like
us down
in the place they think we belong?
So keep going, stay strong, because
it's only when you find you've got nothing to prove
that you truly hit your groove
and all these people, here in this room
They know you're a poet

If you wake with a start
in a cold night sweat
chasing the tail of a dream
you're already forgetting
no energy to rise,
keep it bottled tight inside
strength sapped
bogged down jammed up
crammed between the cracks
yawning crawling upside down
one step sideways
two steps back
no steps forward
slipping falling
let loose a shallow sigh
peel back the lids
of your rain tapped eyes
peer at the dome of a dusky sky
the universe a broken pot
patchwork cloud kintsugi
flooding filling golden gaps
stretch to push your fingers through

stand on tiptoes try to touch
reach too far too soon
thrown back
by shaking sudden thunderclaps
swirling windstorm paper stacks
torn away unfolding
ripped apart
picked up replaced
dropped back at the start
adrift with no rudder
alone in the dark
cast up upon a shattered shore
silently shuddering
a sense you've been here once before
or maybe twice or maybe more
Asking yourself what am I doing this for?
Why am I here what is the reason?
Understand this:
you're pushing at an open door
this is your season
all you ever needed
was to believe in yourself

you are a poet

you *are* a poet

you
    are
       a
         poet

the antithesis
to all-or-nothing-thinking
no thinking at all

# THE PHYSICS OF LOVE AND LOSS

love's first lightning bolt
that sudden urge to step out
in front of a train

## Ghosted (1)

You never got back to me
2 blue ticks
3 days ago...

I get the message

it didn't flutter
until it was discarded
his crêpe paper heart

# Constance

At school, I was taught that there are universal constants.
Gravity.
The speed of light in a vacuum.
Planck's constant.
The elementary charge.

At university I learned that physical constants take
many dimensional forms,
and that the fine-structure constant
which characterises the strength of electromagnetic
interaction
is dimensionless

I forgot all this when I went to work –
you don't need that kind of knowledge in most jobs.

But there was another constant I didn't forget.
One I never needed to learn,
because it was self-evident.
That constant was you.
But now you are gone,
and the fabric of the universe
is torn asunder.

coming through in waves
or particles, I can't tell
October sunlight

# Foreshore

It took three days
once the guests had departed
for the wind to drop.

In accordance with your wishes,
I carried you
down to the foreshore
and left you there
beneath a seething mercury sky
among the worm casts and razor clams.

No grave no
headstone just
mud, weed, wind
and cold relentless tide.

Lately
as winter comes around again
I find myself returning, now and then
to watch sandpipers skittering
among the jagged jutting ribs
of rotten boat carcasses.
The low sun, glinting on weed-slick stones.
Greenshanks and oystercatchers in stark silhouette
strutting, probing
sending delicate shockwaves
across tungsten clouds
on a burnished mirror.

And finally, I understand.
You had no need
of a headstone or memorial plaque,

because you are here.
Resting in the mud and reeds.
Carried back and forth
by the endless wind and tide.

Here, at the foreshore.
Your atoms incorporated
into the feathers and flesh
of the birds
whose names you taught me.

this cluttered study
has never been emptier
Dad's armchair

## Poem for the person I smiled at on the train because I was residually happy from seeing a rainbow

Eye roll
Window
    to the soul
In one split second
I'm told
Every
   thing
 I       need
     to
       know

string theory lesson
she plucks threads on her sweater
and I unravel

# Ghosted (2)

No second date.
She saw right through him.

little heartbreaker
April, fresh from the shower
in a sky-blue robe

## Blackout

However hard you run, the world spins faster.
Sometimes there is no choice but to embrace the darkness.

Pallid pools of candlelight offer no comfort.
Night is inevitable, enveloping all.

Will you succumb easily, a drowning child blithely
swallowed by the sea?
Or will you turn and stand to face it down?

Some fights have to be fought.
Some things are worth dying for.

My mother's womb was dark.
Even there, *safety* was an illusion.

letting go her hand
as though it never happened
the end of summer

# EARTHBOUND

futile gestures
flags forlornly fluttering
climate conference

## Diplomatic Bag

Can you fight your way out of a paper bag
when paper's made of trees?
Chop it down
Rip
    it
        up
until you cannot breathe.

light pollution
the wishes we never made
on falling stars

# Pond~~life~~

Brittle withies linger all along
the fringes of a desiccated pond.

Reed beds rustle, a whispered lament...

Where once stood verdant fronds,
now broken stalks, dry and snapped.

Thickets growing thinner,
sun-baked mudflats, leather-skinned and cracked.

Dragonflies dart no more, like bright neon needles
stitching the hem of a glittering shore.

Long gone, the willow warbler's song,
choked by smoke from belching stacks.

Crows hop back and forth beside the road,
picking clean their brethren's bones.

Monstrous trucks lumber by,
their thunderous growls so casually thrown.

Time's spell, cast by a withered wand.
Sky slate grey, overcast.

The earth shudders.

little honeybee
carrying all our futures
on dusty shoulders

# The Green Man's Prayer

In the cloister he must slumber
Bound to stone by man's design
Until the wheel returns to summer

Through centuries of wanton plunder,
the burning of his faithful wives
In the cloister he must slumber

The screaming wind, the claps of thunder
shall not disturb his resting ire
Until the wheel returns to summer

While men run rampant, unencumbered
and empires rise, and fall, and rise
In the cloister he must slumber

Moss grows moister, tendrils softly clamber
Ivy climbs the lofty spire
And so, the wheel returns to summer

Till roots find cracks to shiver stone asunder
Till dawn's light rests upon his eye
In the cloister he must slumber
From summer's ashes he shall rise

it doesn't end here
in the charred wake of wildfire
a green fern unfurls

# Acknowledgements

Thank you to Clark, a true sensei and modern-day master of the haiku form.

To the friends who have shared the journey with me, especially (in no particular order) Mariya, Dana, Valerie, Sandra, Becka, Susan, Jaeni and Suzanne.

Finally to Anna and the team at Cheltenham Poetry Festival, for supporting and encouraging me when I was finding it hard to believe in myself.

Other anthologies and collections available from Stairwell Books

For further information please contact rose@stairwellbooks.com
www.stairwellbooks.co.uk
@stairwellbooks

Milton Keynes UK
Ingram Content Group UK Ltd.
UKHW020802310324
440087UK00001B/15